Spiders
and Their
Webs

Darlyne A. Murawski

 NATIONAL GEOGRAPHIC

Washington, D.C.

Introduction

You can find spider webs just about everywhere you look—in forests, deserts, gardens, even underwater. About 13,000 of the 38,000 known species of spiders make webs to capture insects and other small prey.

Spider webs are made of silk threads. Young and female spiders are usually the web builders. Spider silk is liquid when it is inside glands in the spider's abdomen. It becomes threadlike as it is drawn out of tiny openings in the spinnerets on the bottom of the spider's abdomen. A thread of spider silk is stronger than a thread of steel of the same thickness. Some silk is stretchy, like a rubber band. Some is sticky. In fact, spiders can make as many as seven different kinds of silk. Each kind is used for a different purpose, such as making egg cases or wrapping prey (like the Argiope, left).

When an insect gets stuck in the threads, the spider attacks. To keep their prey from escaping, spiders injects venom from their fangs. They may also wrap prey tightly in silk. Most spiders have teeth to chew an insect's hard exoskeleton. They spit up juices that turn the prey's insides to liquid so they can drink it.

Spiders deserve our respect. They control insect populations and, in turn, become food for birds and many other animals. Although most spiders aren't harmful to us, a few species deliver a bite that can be painful or even deadly. With spiders, it's best for their safety and ours to LOOK BUT DON'T TOUCH.

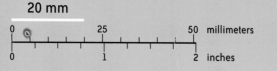

Argiope (ar-JIE-oh-pee)

This orb web (photograph, left) is the work of a young Argiope spider. By sitting in the middle of the squiggly web decoration, the spider can hide from birds and other enemies. These threads also  help the spider catch food. They are made of special silk that is mainly ultraviolet. We can't see this color, but insects can. Some flowers have similar ultraviolet patterns. That means a bee or wasp that sees this design thinks it's going to get a sweet treat. Instead, it gets stuck in the web. The spider quickly wraps its meal tightly in lots of silk. Then bites it with its fangs. With Argiope the rule is wrap first, bite later.

DID YOU KNOW?

Each species of Argiope makes its own kind of web decoration, ranging from lacy designs to X shapes. Some change the pattern when they make a new web.

SPIDER FACTS

🕷 **Scientific name:** *Nephila clavipes* (Family: Tetragnathidae, long-jawed orb weavers)

🕷 **Common names:** golden orb weaver, golden silk spider, banana spider

🕷 **Body size:** 24 to 40 mm (adult females; males are much smaller)

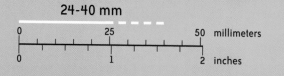

24-40 mm

🕷 **Habitats:** forests and clearings in northern South America, in Central America, and in the southern United States (mainly Florida and Texas)

🕷 **Food:** mainly a variety of flying insects, such as moths, flies, and bees, but has also been known to eat small birds and frogs

Golden Orb Weaver

This huge spider (photograph, left) is a golden orb weaver. That tiny spider with her is her mate! Her web can be three feet wide or larger. It is strong enough to last for several days. This spider can choose the color of silk she makes to spin her webs: gold for webs in sunny places; white for webs in shady places. What looks like drops of water on the web (small photograph, left) are really glue drops. When an insect, like the bee in the art, flies into the web, it gets stuck in a sticky mess. The spider runs out and bites it with her long fangs. She can eat the insect right away or wrap it in silk and store it in her web for later.

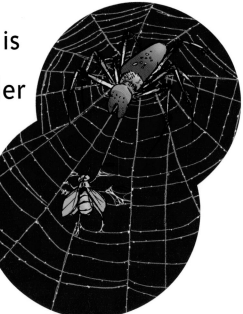

DID YOU KNOW? Spiders know if a visitor is the right size to eat by how much the web shakes when it lands. Luckily, male golden orb weavers are too small to be mistaken for food.

SPIDER FACTS

🕷 **Scientific name:** This is one of about 50 species in the genus *Deinopis* (Family: Deinopidae)

🕷 **Common names:** ogre-faced spider, net-casting spider

🕷 **Body size:** about 25 mm (adult females; males are smaller)

25 mm

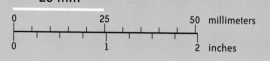

🕷 **Habitats:** vegetation in the lowest level of rain forests in Central America and northern South America

🕷 **Food:** small- to medium-size crawling or flying insects, such as caterpillars and crickets

Ogre-Faced Spider

The ogre-faced spider does its hunting at night. It has large eyes that help it see in the dark. The spider hangs upside-down from silk threads that are attached to branches. It holds a net-

like web between its front legs (large photograph, left). When something good to eat, like a caterpillar, comes along, the spider tosses the web over it (small photograph, left). The prey sticks to the web's Velcro-like threads. The spider bites its prey then spits up juices that "melt" the soft parts of the insect's body. The spider can hold its meal with its front legs and spin a new web with its hind legs—all at the same time!

DID YOU KNOW?

To keep from being seen by birds and other enemies during the day, the ogre-faced spider stretches out to make itself look like a twig (art, above).

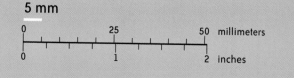

SPIDER FACTS

- **Scientific name:** *Theridion grallator* (Family: Theridiiae)

- **Common name:** Hawaiian happy-faced spider

- **Body size:** up to 5 mm (adult females; males are smaller)

- **Habitats:** underside of leaves in Hawaiian wet forests, from Oahu to the big island of Hawaii

- **Food:** small insects, such as young leafhoppers and fruit flies

Hawaiian Happy-Faced Spider

You have to use a magnifying glass to see this tiny yellow spider with the big grin on her abdomen. She makes a messy little web in a shallow dip on the underside of a leaf. The spider uses her web to protect her eggs and to store food. When a small insect visits her leaf, she springs into action. With her hind legs, she pulls silk from her spinnerets and tosses it over her prey. Then, she reels it in. After she wraps her meal in silk, she tucks it in the web next to her eggs. When she gets hungry, she'll eat it. After her eggs hatch, she'll use the web as a nursery and find food for her babies for a few months.

DID YOU KNOW? Not all happy-faced spiders have a smiley-face pattern on their abdomens. Some have other expressions or just an abstract design.

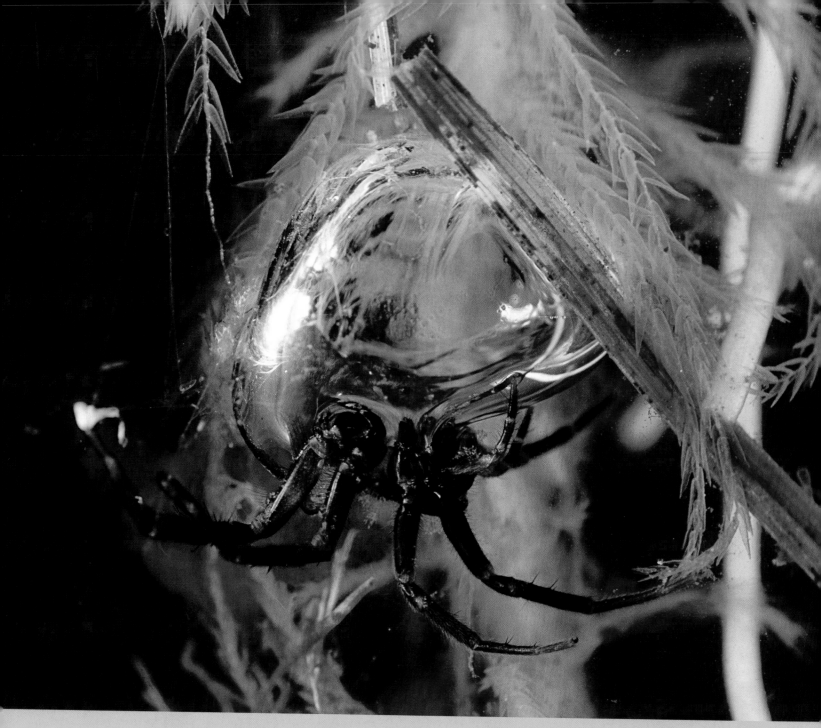

SPIDER FACTS

* **Scientific name:** *Argyroneta aquatica* (Family: Argyronetidae)

* **Common name:** water spider

* **Body size:** about 13 mm (adult males; females are slightly smaller)

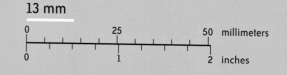

13 mm

0   25   50   millimeters

0   1   2   inches

* **Habitats:** ponds, quiet streams, and shallow lakes in northern and central Europe and in central Asia

* **Food:** a variety of small aquatic invertebrates, such as tadpoles and baby fish

Water Spider

This kind of spider lives underwater, but it needs air to breathe. To solve this problem, it builds an air-bubble house. First it attaches strands of silk to the leaves and stems of water plants. Then it fills the space with a netlike web. The spider makes several trips to the surface. Each time, a bubble of air sticks to its hairy abdomen. The spider carries the air bubbles back to its web and brushes them off. The air makes the web swell up like a balloon. The spider swims outside its house to catch its food, then drags it inside to eat. That's where the spider mates and lays its eggs, too.

DID YOU KNOW? Water spiders must swim to the surface often to get new air for their webs. The new air is rich in oxygen, which the spider needs to breathe.

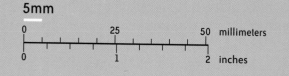

Social Spiders

Some spiders live together in groups. They are called social spiders. Thousands of these spiders work together to make a web that can be as big as a garbage truck! The web has a sheet of silk across the bottom. Lots of long lines attach the sheet to the branches of trees and shrubs, as shown in the art above. These lines "trip" flying insects. They fall down and are caught in the sheet. The tiny spiders you see in the photograph (left) are busy attacking a katydid that flew into their web. By working together, social spiders can catch and eat insects that are many times larger than they are.

DID YOU KNOW? Instead of making a new web when it gets damaged or dirty, these spiders work together to repair and clean the one they have.

* **Scientific name:** family Theridioso-matidae; genus and species can't be determined from this photograph.

* **Common names:** ray spider, ray orb weaver, cone web spider

* **Body size:** about 3 mm (adult females; males are smaller)

3 mm

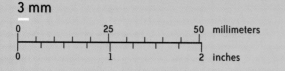

* **Habitats:** dark, damp locations near streams and in shaded woods. Most species live in the tropics, but some can be found in the U.S., Europe, and Asia. This photograph was taken in a Costa Rican rain forest.

* **Food:** small flying insects, such as flies, moths, and beetles

Ray Spider

The ray spider (left) makes an orb web that it uses like a slingshot to snag a meal. With its front legs, the spider pulls on a silk thread that draws the web back (Step 1). When the spider senses food is near,

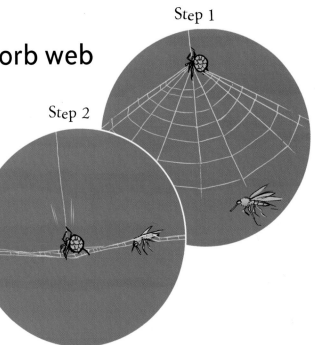

Step 1

Step 2

it loosens its grip on the thread. The web springs out and catches the insect in the sticky, spiral threads (Step 2). Then the spider runs across the web and grabs its prey. Special hairs and claws on the spider's feet keep it from getting stuck in its own web. This spider can use its web a few times before it has to build a new one.

DID YOU KNOW? You can trick this spider by rubbing your thumb against your fingertips under its web. Sensing something is near, the spider will release its web.

SPIDER FACTS

❋ **Scientific name:** family Theridiidae; genus and species cannot be determined from this photograph.

❋ **Common names:** cobweb spider, comb-footed spider, gumfoot spider

❋ **Body size:** 2–3mm (adult females; males are slightly smaller)

❋ **Habitats:** nooks and crannies in vegetation, under rocks and around buildings

❋ **Food:** small crawling and flying insects, such as springtails and flies

3 mm

0	25	50	millimeters
0	1	2	inches

Cobweb Spider

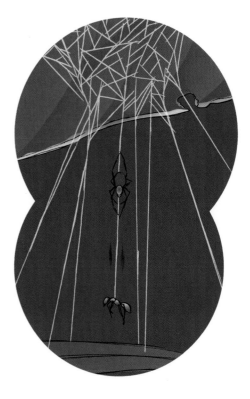

The spider that made this messy-looking web (photograph, left) is called a cobweb spider. That red dot in the middle is the spider hanging upside-down. It's waiting for a meal. It traps insects with silk threads attached to the lower leaf.

They are sticky near the bottom. When an ant or some other kind of small insect touches one of these threads, it gets stuck. The line breaks away from the leaf. Like a yo-yo, it springs up, carrying the insect toward the spider. The spider flings more silk around the insect to make sure it can't get away. Then the spider delivers a deadly bite and sucks its prey dry.

DID YOU KNOW? Cobweb spiders are some of the easiest spiders to find. Chances are you have some in your house or in your garage.

SPIDER FACTS

🕷 **Scientific name:** *Tengella radiata* (Family: Tengellidae)

🕷 **Common name:** Tengellid funnel-web spider (This is one of many species of spiders that make funnel webs.)

🕷 **Body size:** about 20 mm (adult females; males are smaller)

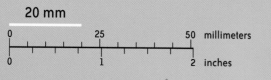

🕷 **Habitats:** along banks and near the base of buttressed trees in rain forests in Costa Rica

🕷 **Food:** small- to medium-size flying insects, such as moths and grasshoppers

Tengellid Funnel-Web Spider

The Tengellid funnel-web spider made the silky nets decorating the hollows of this tree (large photograph, left). These webs are invisible to insects. You can see them because I dusted them with powder so they would show up in the photograph. The spider hides in a silk-lined tunnel connected to the outer part of its web (art, above). When a moth or other insect flies into the web, the spider attacks. It races out of its tunnel, jumps on its prey, and bites it. Poison from the spider paralyzes the insect so it can't escape. Then the spider drags it into the safety of its tunnel, where it can eat in peace.

DID YOU KNOW? Tiny spiders and bugs live in the funnel web and scrounge a free meal by feeding on the spider's leftovers, like the wing in the small photograph (left).

Other Uses for Spider Silk

All spiders can spin silk threads, but not all spiders make webs. Let's look at some of the other uses for spider silk in nature.

Egg Cases: Spiders use a special kind of silk to make sacs to hold their eggs. The spider shown here made three egg cases. Each one is bigger than the spider and has between 6 and 12 eggs.

Retreats: Look closely, and you can see the eyes and front legs of a tarantula sticking out from its shelter on this tree. Tarantulas build silk retreats to rest in during the day and to hide from their enemies.

Fishing Lines: The tiny tropical *Wendilgarda* spider strings a strand of silk across a stream. Then it hangs "fishing lines" that attach to the water's surface and catch passing water striders.

Hunting Tool: Bolas spiders attract male moths by mimicking the odors of female moths. To catch their prey, they swing a silk line with a glue drop on the end. This spider has caught one moth and is hunting for another.

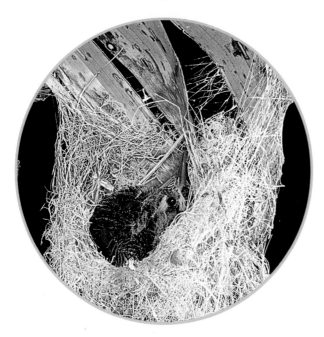

Bird Nests: Hummingbirds steal bits of spider web to make their nests stronger. To fasten the nest to a leaf, adults take strands of silk in their beaks and fly in circles around it.

Step 1

Put one sock inside the other to make a double-thick bag.

Step 2

Fill the bag with cornstarch or talcum powder.

Step 3

Close the opening by tying a knot in the top of the "bag."

Activity

Finding webs is easy on a foggy or dew-covered morning because the water drops reveal the silk threads. But you'll have to wait to see the spider at work. That's because a spider can't catch a meal until its web dries out and becomes invisible again. But when conditions are good for the spider, you might have a hard time finding webs. Here's a trick biologists use to make spider webs visible. (I used this trick to photograph the webs on the cover and pages 18, 20, 22, and 25 top). Here's what you'll need:

- ✳ 2 socks
- ✳ 1 cup of cornstarch or talcum powder

Now follow Steps 1–6, below.

Remember: Spiders can't capture prey when their webs become visible. Sometimes you can gently blow the dust off the web so the spider can go on using it. Usually, though, the spider will abandon the web and make a new one. So, don't dust the new web. Once you know where to look for webs in your area, you can go back and watch the spiders at work—eating, repairing torn webs, and making new ones.

Step 4

Hold the bag next to a spider web (not over the top of it) as shown in the photograph.

Step 5

Pat the bag gently to force powder out of it onto the web. Hint: Stand upwind so the air carries the powder onto the web.

Step 6

Keep patting the bag until the web is lightly dusted.

When I landed a National Geographic assignment to photograph spiders and their webs, I knew I had a big challenge in front of me. Most spider webs are nearly invisible. This means they are both hard to find and difficult to photograph. This is why wherever I went, I hired an assistant who could help me find the spiders I was looking for. A spider specialist taught me how to dust webs (the same trick I shared with you on pages 26–27).

I learned to search an area slowly and carefully, looking around the base of trees, over streams, between leaves, under rocks—any place a spider might choose to set its silk trap. I found many webs, but to see a spider spring into action, I often had to wait patiently for hours—day and night.

The rain forest is a rich hunting ground for spiders. It is full of insects and other small prey that spiders like to eat. That's the good news. The bad news is that wearing insect repellent could keep the spiders and their prey away. I chose to work in areas where mosquito-borne diseases aren't a problem. The thrill of photographing some little-known spider behavior makes you forget about any discomfort. In Costa Rica I observed something few people have seen: a golden orb weaver (page 8) eating a tree frog. When I checked on the spider the next morning, she looked like she'd swallowed a Ping-Pong ball!

When I'm on assignment, I try to be prepared for everything, but some things you just can't plan for. One evening while I was photographing a Tengellid funnel-web spider (page 22), I saw a large moth fly into its web. The spider came galloping out of its tunnel and pounced on the struggling moth. Suddenly, the moth escaped from the web with the spider still attached to it. (Sometimes moths and butterflies can free themselves from a web by shedding the scales on their wings.) Attracted by the light in my headlamp, it flew right into my face— several times. Luckily, the spider didn't bite me. On another night, I was kneeling on the ground to photograph the ogre-faced spider (page 10) when I felt something brush past my knees. Not wanting to be disturbed, I finished snapping the picture. Then I looked down and saw a deadly poisonous coral snake slithering by. I shot straight up in the air and leaped backward. You can bet my nerves were frazzled!

Being persistent is important in this business. When I shot the tarantula retreat (page 24), I wanted to see what it looked like on the inside. So I attached a foot-long skinny lens called an endoscope to my camera, climbed up a ladder, and stuck the lens inside the opening. The tarantula raised its fangs and front legs to threaten me. In the viewfinder it looked HUGE. I screamed and fell backward off the ladder. After I caught my breath, I climbed back up, determined to get my picture. My endurance paid off. The photograph was published in NATIONAL GEOGRAPHIC (August 2003, page 45).

I encourage you to have adventures of your own finding spiders and their webs. Cobweb spiders might be good for starters. Examine tiny spiders with a magnifying glass. Try dusting a few webs. Watch a spider make an orb web, then design your own web on paper. I hope you have as much fun learning about spiders as I do.

Darlyne Murawski

Orb-weaving spider *Gasteracantha cancriformis*

What's it mean?

Abdomen - the hind part of the spider's body that contains the silk glands.

Biologist - a person who studies live organisms

Egg case - the silk sac that a spider makes to protect her eggs

Exoskeleton - the hard outer covering on the body of an insect or other animal

Family - a group of species or genera (plural of genus) related by common traits and common ancestry; a category used to classify organisms

Fangs - a pair of needlelike teeth on the tip of a spider's jaws through which the spider can inject venom

Genus - one or more related species; a category used to classify organisms that ranks between family and species

Insects - animals without backbones that have a segmented body including a head (with antennae, compound eyes and up to 3 simple eyes), a thorax (with 6 legs and wings), and an abdomen

Invertebrates - animals without backbones, including insects and spiders

Mimic - copy, imitate

Orb web - a web that has a spiral pattern of silk threads for catching prey

Paralyze - to immobilize, stun, or keep from moving

Prey - an animal that is eaten by another

Species - a group of related organisms with common ancestry that can produce young of the same kind; a category used to classify organisms

Spiders - animals without backbones that have 2 parts to their body: a cephalothorax (the head and thorax fused together) and an abdomen. Eight legs and usually 8 simple eyes are on the cephalothorax.

Rain forest - a tropical woodland that receives more than a hundred inches of rain each year

Spinnerets - a group of paired organs on the abdomen of a spider that spin silk into threads

Books and Magazines

Conniff, Richard and Darlyne Murawski (photographer). "Deadly Silk," NATIONAL GEOGRAPHIC, August 2001, pp. 30–45.

Dewey, Jennifer Owings. *Spiders Near and Far.* NY: Dutton, 1993.

Facklam, Margery and Alan Male (illustrator). *Spiders and Their Web Sites.* NY: Little Brown and Company, 2001.

Glaser, Linda and Gay W. Holland (illustrator). *Spectacular Spiders.* NY: Millbrook Press, 1999.

Levi, Herbert W. and Lorna R. Levi. *Spiders and Their Kin, A Golden Guide*®. NY: St. Martin's Press, 1990.

Parsons, Alexandra. *Amazing Spiders.* NY: Random House, 1990.

Simon, Seymour. *Spiders.* NY: HarperCollins, 2003.

Winter, Yvonne and Karren Lloyd-Jones (illustrator). *Spiders Spin Webs.* Watertown, MA: Charlesbridge, 1998.

Web Sites

The Arachnology Home Page: http://www.arachnology.org

University of Kentucky Entomology for Kids: http://www.uky.edu/Agriculture/entomology/ythfacts/stories/spidrweb.htm

Worldwide (Spider) Webs: http://www.conservation.state.mo.us/conmag/1996/decoi/1.html

DEDICATION: To Elsa and Suzanne, and to the appreciation of nature's diversity

ACKNOWLEDGMENTS: Many thanks to reviewers Herbert W. Levi and Catherine L. Craig, and to all who provided information and field assistance including: William G. Eberhard, Laura Leibens Perger, Steven L. Montgomery, Denis Chavarría, Per Stadel Nielsen, and Paul Tufiño.

Published by the National Geographic Society

1145 17th Street N.W.

Washington, D.C. 20036-4688

Book design by Octavo Designs. Illustrations by Mark Burrier.
Text is set in Bailey Sans ITC and Garamouche, with title type in Strawhouse.

One of the world's largest nonprofit scientific and educational organizations, the National Geographic Society was founded in 1888 "for the increase and diffusion of geographic knowledge." Fulfilling this mission, the Society educates and inspires millions every day through its magazines, books, television programs, videos, maps and atlases, research grants, the National Geographic Bee, teacher workshops, and innovative classroom materials. The Society is supported through membership dues, charitable gifts, and income from the sale of its educational products. This support is vital to National Geographic's mission to increase global understanding and promote conservation of our planet through exploration, research, and education.

For more information, please call 1-800-NGS LINE (647-5463) or write to the following address:

National Geographic Society

1145 17th Street N.W.

Washington, D.C. 20036-4688 U.S.A.

Visit the Society's Web site at www.nationalgeographic.com.

Front cover: An *Eriophora* spider waits for prey at the hub of its five-foot-high orb web.

Library of Congress Cataloging-in-Publication Data

Murawski, Darlyne.
Spiders and their webs / written by Darlyne A. Murawski
p. cm.
Includes bibliographical references.
ISBN 0-7922-6979-9 (harcover edition); 0-7922-6994-2 (reinforced library binding)
1. Spiders—Juvenile literature. 2. Spider webs—Juvenile literature. I. Title.
QL458.4.M87 2004
595.4'4—dc22   2004000397

Printed in Mexico